2/10

BKm

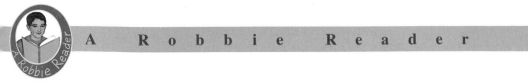
How To Convince Your Parents You Can...

Care For A Puppy

Michelle Medlock Adams

Mitchell Lane

PUBLISHERS

P.O. Box 196
Hockessin, Delaware 19707
Visit us on the web: www.mitchelllane.com
Comments? email us: mitchelllane@mitchelllane.com

Mitchell Lane
PUBLISHERS

Copyright © 2010 by Mitchell Lane Publishers. All rights reserved. No part of this book may be reproduced without written permission from the publisher. Printed and bound in the United States of America.

Printing   1   2   3   4   5   6   7   8   9

A Robbie Reader/How to Convince Your Parents You Can...

Care for a Kitten
Care for a Pet Bunny
Care for a Pet Chameleon
Care for a Pet Chimpanzee
Care for a Pet Chinchilla
Care for a Pet Ferret
Care for a Pet Guinea Pig
Care for a Pet Hamster
Care for a Pet Hedgehog
Care for a Pet Horse

Care for a Pet Mouse
Care for a Pet Parrot
Care for a Pet Racing Pigeon
Care for a Pet Snake
Care for a Pet Sugar Glider
Care for a Pet Tarantula
Care for a Pet Wolfdog
Care for a Potbellied Pig
Care for a Puppy
Care for a Wild Chincoteague Pony

Library of Congress Cataloging-in-Publication Data
Adams, Michelle Medlock.
  Care for a puppy / by Michelle Medlock Adams.
      p. cm. — (A Robbie reader. How to convince your parents you can—)
  Includes bibliographical references and index.
  ISBN 978-1-58415-802-8 (library bound)
 1. Puppies—Juvenile literature. I. Title. II. Title: How to convince your parents you can—care for a puppy.
  SF426.5.A335 2010
  636.7'07—dc22
                                                                    2009027353

ABOUT THE AUTHOR: Michelle Medlock Adams is an award-winning journalist and  author, earning top honors from the Associated Press, the Society of Professional Journalists, the Sunday and Features Editors, and the Hoosier State Press Association. Since graduating with a journalism degree from Indiana University in 1991, Michelle has worked as a reporter for a daily newspaper in Southern Indiana; acted as a stringer for the Associated Press in Indiana; written full time for a worldwide ministry's website and magazine; and authored 41 books. She is the proud owner of three miniature long-haired dachshunds: Maddie, Miller, and Mollie. Her website is www.michellemedlockadams.com.

Michelle and Mollie

PUBLISHER'S NOTE: The facts on which this story is based have been thoroughly researched. Documentation of such research is listed on page 30. While every possible effort has been made to ensure accuracy, the publisher will not assume liability for damages caused by inaccuracies in the data, and makes no warranty on the accuracy of the information contained herein.

TABLE OF CONTENTS

Words in bold type can be found in the glossary.

This cute yellow Labrador retriever puppy is not only lovable but very smart. The Labrador retriever is one of the prime breeds selected as guide and rescue dogs.

Chapter One 1

OPERATION: GET A PUPPY!

Okay, so you *really* want a puppy of your own, right? But you're not sure you can convince your mom or dad that you're ready to be an official pet owner. Well, don't worry. This book is designed to teach you cool and useful information about puppies so that you can prove to your parents you will be a responsible master to your new puppy. We'll call this mission Operation: Get a Puppy!

First, you'll need to be armed with lots of reasons that a puppy would be a good addition to your already busy life. So here is a "Top Ten Reasons I Need a Puppy" list to share with your parents. (Feel free to change it a little to make it sound more like you.)

Top Ten Reasons I Need a Puppy

10. A puppy is a great friend, so you won't ever have to feel lonely again.
9. A puppy will help you get more exercise, because you'll need to walk him and play with him every day.
8. A puppy will keep you from spending so much time on the computer or in front of the TV, because you'll be too busy playing with your new puppy.
7. A puppy will build your confidence, because you'll learn that you are good at taking care of your dog.
6. A puppy will teach you about loyalty, because dogs are extremely loyal.
5. Your feet will never be cold again, because a puppy is furry and can keep your feet nice and cozy when you tuck your toes under his belly.
4. A puppy is a great alarm system, because she will bark whenever someone is coming or danger is nearby.
3. A puppy helps keep the floor very clean, because he will lick up the crumbs you drop when you eat a snack. Yum!
2. A puppy will make you feel safe, because dogs have a great desire to protect the people they love.
1. A puppy will grow into a dog who will always be your best friend. After all, dogs have been called "Man's Best Friend" for many years.

There you go! You have a Top Ten list to present to your parents. Now you need to learn more about taking care of puppies, and you need to figure out the best kind of puppy for your family. Some dogs are very hyper. Others are more laid back. Some dog breeds are known for being very smart. Other breeds are known for their feisty attitudes. Some little puppies stay little, but others get very, very big! And some dogs need lots and lots of room to run around outside, so you might want to talk to Mom or Dad about building a fence or putting in a buried electric fence, made by companies such as **Invisible Fence®**, to keep your dog safe. You don't want your friend to run away, right? Whatever kind of puppy you choose, the most important thing to remember is this: Your puppy will love you no matter what; and you need to return that love.

fun FACTS

It's a good idea to adopt or buy a breed of dog that your family already knows a little about. If your mom grew up with a dachshund, then you'll know what to expect from that kind of dog.

Chihuahua puppies love to be cuddled. In fact, they enjoy the company of humans over the company of other animals.

Chapter Two

WHAT ARE PUPPIES LIKE?

Canis lupus familiaris is the Latin term for *dog*. Dogs come from the same family (canines) as foxes, jackals, and wolves, which are all hunters.

How big will your puppy grow? That depends on the breed. Saint Bernards grow twenty-eight inches tall and weigh 135 pounds. Compare that with a Chihuahua. These tiny dogs grow only five inches tall and weigh six pounds when full grown. If you live in an apartment, you might need to get a smaller dog like a Chihuahua, a Pomeranian, or a dachshund. But if you live on a farm with lots and lots of room for running, you could have a larger dog such as a Labrador retriever or even a Saint Bernard. You also might want to find a mutt (a mixed-breed dog) that is the right size for your home. Mixed-breed dogs make lovely pets.

How long do dogs live? This depends on the breed and on how well you take care of your dog. Saint

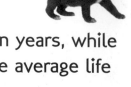

Bernards might live only seven to eleven years, while Chihuahuas may live to be eighteen! The average life span for a dog is about twelve years.

It's a well-known fact that every dog year equals about seven years of a human's life, so when your puppy turns three years old, he is really twenty-one years old in human years.

Once your puppy is old enough, you'll want to get your dog **spayed** or **neutered**. This is just part of being a **responsible** pet owner. Dogs instinctively want to breed. That means they want to make more puppies. If you get too many puppies in one household, it could be very expensive and chaotic. Your mom and dad probably won't like that. You can either get a dog that's already been spayed or neutered at the local humane society, or get your puppy fixed right away.

Having a growing dog in your house is like having a two-year-old around. Do you have a little sister or

*fun*FACTS

You might want to buy your dog at a neighborhood shelter, from someone you know, or from someone a friend recommends. That way, you'll be sure to get a dog that is healthy.

Saint Bernards are big and lovable and very trainable. They originally come from Switzerland and can be trained to be rescue dogs. They are part of the hound grouping.

Top Ten AKC* Breeds

1. Labrador Retriever

2. Yorkshire Terrier

3. German Shepherd

4. Golden Retriever

5. Beagle

6. Boxer

7. Dachshund

8. Poodle

9. Shih Tzu

10. Bulldog

*AKC = American Kennel Club

brother? If you do, then you know that little children get into everything! Your puppy will be the same way. He might even chew your new pair of shoes if you don't watch him carefully. You'll need to be patient with your puppy while you're training him.

Does your whole family want a dog? If your sister is scared of dogs, it will be hard to talk your parents into getting one. If your dad is allergic to dogs, he will be tough to convince, too. It's smart to talk to your parents or guardians before you decide that a puppy is the perfect pet for you. If you're even a little unsure of which type of dog to choose, you might want to go to your local humane society to see which dogs grow big, which ones shed their fur more than others, which ones are more hyper, etc. If you buy a **hyperactive** dog, she will need lots more exercise than some of the laid-back dogs. Are you okay with taking her outside to run and play?

And are you okay with taking her on walks to different places, so she can smell new things? Dogs like that. Also, is there a safe, fenced-in place where you can take her and throw a ball for her to fetch until she gets tired? Many cities have dog parks, so check out your area for those special places for pooches.

Thinking about these things can make the difference between a good decision and a disaster— for you and your whole family. You want to choose a puppy that your whole family will love and accept.

Labrador retrievers love to fetch things, and they love to chew anything and everything. If you choose a Lab as your new puppy, make sure you buy some special chew toys for it.

CHOOSING YOUR PUPPY AND BRINGING IT HOME

Before you bring your puppy home, you'll need to puppy-proof your house. Ask your mom or dad to cover exposed wires. You can help them put the antique furniture in the attic. Carefully put all household cleaners away and hide the garbage—under the sink or in the basement or pantry. Have your mom or dad spray all wood with bitter apple. It will keep your dog from chewing on your furniture, and it's safe for the dog. Put all houseplants up high—dogs love chewing on the leaves and digging!

Where can you buy a puppy? Almost anywhere, and at any price. Your neighbors might have puppies they're giving away, or you might pay $1,000 or more for a purebred pup. Ask your parents how much they are willing to spend, so you'll know where to start your search.

You can find puppies at your local humane society, animal shelter, or pound; your neighbor's

house; a pet store; online; through a breeder's listing online or in newspapers; or through a purebred rescue organization.

Remember when choosing your pup, you should buy one that is eight to ten weeks old and has been **weaned.** That way, he'll be an easygoing puppy and won't miss his mom too much.

Second, when you look for puppies, you'll want to pick the puppy that gets along with his brothers and sisters the very best, so observe how the puppies interact with one another. Watch them for several minutes before you interrupt their play. Next, talk in a friendly voice and call the puppies to you. Bend down when you talk to them so they won't be scared of you.

Dogs love to be talked to by their owners, and they respond to your tone of voice. If you sound excited, your pup will know you are ready to play!

When you take your puppy home, he may miss his brothers and sisters. To prevent too much sadness in your pup, allow him and his canine family to play with a chew toy for a while. Then when you take your pup home, also take that chew toy. It will smell like his siblings and make him feel happy.

You look huge to a puppy! Usually, one specific puppy will seem friendlier toward you. It's as if that puppy knows you're supposed to be his new owner. See which puppy comes to you and wants to play. That's your puppy.

When you play with your new puppy, have fun! You can tug on an old sock with him, play with a tennis ball, or just crawl around on all fours. Remember to be gentle, though. You don't want to injure your pup by accident.

Also, you'll need to be careful when handling your pup. When you pick up the puppy, gently hold him under his belly with one hand, and hold his hind end with the other.

Once you've made your choice, it's time to go home and get started.

Find out what kind of food your puppy was fed at her former home and use that same brand of food when feeding her at your house. A change in diet can upset a puppy's tummy.

TAKING CARE OF YOUR NEW BEST FRIEND

So you've brought your puppy home. What now? Your puppy will no longer be getting milk from his or her mother, so you will need to buy puppy food. You, his owner, should feed him. That way, he'll know you're the boss, or in doggy language, the alpha dog, the leader of the dog pack. This establishes **authority**, something that you'll need with your new puppy.

When you first get your puppy, feed him four times a day in small amounts. The amount of food you feed your pup will depend on his age and weight, so read the back of the dog food bag to figure out exactly how much. When he is six months old, you can cut out one feeding. And when your dog is eleven months old, feed him twice a day for the rest of his life.

You should give him puppy food until he's about a year and a half old. After that, switch to adult formula dog food. Make sure that you feed him and

give him water every day at the same times of day. Dogs like routines.

It's a bad idea to give your puppy people food. He'll get used to begging, might get sick (you'll have to clean up his mess—he's your dog!), and may gain weight from eating people food. It's better to give him dog food and some dog treats—but not too many.

Grooming Your Puppy

Brush your dog often. It makes him feel safe, and will help you two **bond**. Use a very soft human brush on him, not a spiky metal comb. A puppy's skin is very sensitive, so be gentle. And talk sweetly to him, saying nice things like, "Good boy," and "Doesn't that feel good?"

When brushing your dog, look for fleas and ticks. Fleas and ticks are bugs that can live in your dog's fur. Gently separate your pup's fur from his skin using your fingers, or brush the fur backward to see if you notice any black specks. Then, using a wet paper towel, wipe away the specks. If they turn red, your dog has fleas. That red stuff is flea dirt. You'd better tell your parents.

Look for ticks, too. As soon as you see a tick, tell your mom or dad. Your parents can pull off ticks with tweezers. If your puppy is covered with ticks, you may need to call the **veterinarian** and schedule a tick dip. It's smart to use a good flea and tick shampoo and check your dog after every trip outside.

You also might want to use a flea collar or drops such as Frontline or K9 Advantix, which will keep ticks and fleas off your dog. The drops are usually applied to the back of the puppy's neck and are available from your vet—but some brands are poisonous to cats, so if you also have a cat, avoid the drops. You can buy flea collars from most stores, and they cost less than the drops.

You'll need to give your dog a bath when he gets dirty, smelly, or whenever your parents tell you to. It's a smart idea to wash your dog outside in a wash bin or in the bathtub. You might need help for this. Brush him first. Then fill up a bucket with warm water and set it aside. Get him wet with warm water, then shampoo his fur with dog shampoo. Be gentle! Rinse him off with the bucket of clean water. If you use the bathtub, close the shower curtain and let him shake

fun FACTS

You might want to ask your vet or groomer to trim your dog's nails until you're a bit older. You have to be super careful that you don't cut the nails too short, or they will bleed.

When you give your dog a bath, put cotton in his or her ears to prevent water from entering the ear canals.

off the water. Let him dry off on a towel in a warm place, like a sunny deck or kitchen. After he's dry, give him another quick brushing—and a treat for being such a good dog.

Keeping Your Puppy Healthy
You will also have to take your puppy to the veterinarian for **vaccinations** (vak-sih-NAY-shuns). Your vet will give your puppy vaccines (vak-SEENS) at six weeks, at fourteen to sixteen weeks, and once a year for the rest of his life. Vaccines work to fight diseases, and will keep your pooch healthy for a lifetime.

Training Your Puppy

As soon as you come home, start training your dog to sit, stay, and lie down. It's best to use one-word commands, like "Sit," "Stay," and "Down." Talk in a firm, sure-of-yourself voice, and practice with your pup two or three times a day for ten minutes at a time. Before you know it, your dog will listen to you, and he will be more fun for the whole family.

Don't try to punish your dog. Instead, praise him every time he does something right. Dogs learn better that way—and they'll learn to trust you.

To potty train your pup, put down newspapers for him to use. Then, when you see him sniffing around or walking in circles, you'll know he needs to go. Hurry and place him on his papers, and say, "Good boy!" when he goes. For smaller dogs, many people train them to go in a litter box, much like kittens do.

You would train the same way as paper training, only you'd put your pooch in the litter box instead of on the papers.

The ultimate goal is for your puppy to do his business outside, either on a walk or in your fenced-in yard. Encourage that behavior and praise him every time he gets it right. Work with him, teaching him to go to the door when he needs to potty outside. Try to use the same words every time you ask: "Potty outside?" Say it over and over, so he will get used to it. Remember to scoop your pup's poop—whether it's in your own yard or your neighbor's, in a park, or on a sidewalk.

Ten Things That Are Deadly to Your Puppy

Keep these things up high. Call your vet immediately if you think your puppy has eaten any of them.

1. Antifreeze (People use antifreeze in cars. It smells and tastes sweet to your dog, but it is fatal.)
2. Tylenol (two regular strength [325 mg] Tylenol can kill a small dog)
3. Chocolate
4. Bleach
5. Watch batteries
6. Moth balls
7. Fabric softener and laundry detergent
8. Mouthwash
9. Peach pits
10. Many kinds of household plants

People food isn't good for dogs—and you definitely don't want to eat any food your pooch has licked.

When you leave for school, or when you go to bed at night, keep your puppy in a crate. Dogs like dens. They feel safe inside a crate. Remember to buy a crate that will fit him when he is fully grown. Put towels around the sides and back of the crate, and put some folded towels, or even a soft blanket, on the bottom. Toss a treat and a few toys inside, and gently place him in the crate. He will feel warm, safe, and happy. You can buy wire mesh crates that the dog can see through, or hard plastic crates that make the dog feel like he's in a den. Just be sure to take him outside if he scratches the crate or whines loudly. That may be his way of telling you he needs to go potty.

Dogs show affection by licking. It's their way of giving someone a kiss. To keep your puppy's breath fresh, brush his or her teeth with special doggie toothpaste at least once a week.

PERFECTING THE PUPPY PITCH TO YOUR PARENTS

Owning a puppy is a wonderful adventure, but it can be a lot of work. Puppies require lots of time. You may have to spend less time playing video games so that you can give your puppy the love and attention he or she needs. Also, you have to train your puppy to potty outside; how to act when meeting new people; how to play without biting; and lots more. It's a big time commitment, so you need to consider that before you bring home a pooch. Will you have time for a puppy in your busy day?

Puppies, like new toys, lose their "newness" very quickly. You have to know in your heart that you'll love this puppy long after the newness has worn off. Will you? Too many people get puppies for Christmas and later decide that a puppy is just too much work, which is why so many humane societies are overcrowded with unwanted animals.

Puppies will probably destroy something you love. Your new pup won't mean to make you mad, but he probably will. Like babies, puppies have to learn what is okay to do and what is not okay to do. While learning those important rules, he may chew up your favorite toy or go potty in your room. Yuck! Will you be patient with your new puppy as he learns?

If you're still reading, you probably still want a puppy. Think of all the reasons you really want one, and practice giving a speech to your parents, listing all those reasons. Convince them that you will be a responsible dog owner. You could say something like, "Mom and Dad, I want to have a puppy because I want to take care of him, love him, and train him. I can hardly wait to walk him, brush him, bathe him, play with him, and take him to the vet. I promise to love him when he's jumping and barking and licking

fun FACTS

Leave your puppy's ID collar on while you bathe him. Some dogs do not like baths and will try to run away. If that happens, his ID collar will help you get him back. You might also decide to use a microchip ID. Ask your vet about this option.

my face. And I promise to love him even if he chews up my favorite pair of shoes.

"I've thought about how busy I am and decided that I want to quit Scouts [or gymnastics or Little League or soccer] so that I will have more time to take care of him after school. I've talked to my brothers and sisters, and we all want a dog. I promise I won't make you sorry that you got me a puppy."

Having a dog can be so much fun, and you're guaranteed to have a best friend that will adore you no matter what! Now that you know what it takes to be a good dog owner, go forth and convince your parents that you're ready for a puppy!

FIND OUT MORE

Books

Hodgson, Sarah. *Puppies For Dummies*. Hoboken, NJ: John Wiley & Sons, 2006.

Meyers, Susan. *Puppies! Puppies! Puppies!* New York: Harry N. Abrams, 2005.

Miles, Ellen. *Shadow* (The Puppy Place). New York, NY: Scholastic Paperbacks, 2007.

Roca, Nuria. *Let's Take Care of Our New Dog*. Hauppauge, NY: Barron's Educational Series, 2006.

Truax, Doug. *Raising Riley: A Kid's First Lab Puppy*. Memphis, TN: Ducks Unlimited, 2004.

Works Consulted

Adamson, Eve. "Nail Clipper Options." *Dog Fancy*, June 2008, p. 22

———. "Your Dog Rolled in What?" *Dog Fancy*, June 2008, p. 22.

"AKC Dog Registration Statistics."
http://www.akc.org/reg/dogreg_stats.cfm

American Kennel Club. *The Complete Dog Book*. 20th ed. New York: Howell Book House, 2006.

DeVito, Carlo, and Amy Ammen. *The Everything Puppy Book: Choosing, Raising, and Training Your Littlest Best Friend*. Avon, MA: Adams Media Corporation, 2002.

Foster, Race. "Puppy House Training." http://www.peteducation.com/article.cfm?c=2+1548&aid=157

Hayner, Lynn M. "Make It Count: Get the Most Out of That Special Dog Time." *Dog Fancy*, January 2008. pp. 34–37.

"How Long Will My Dog Live?" http://www.petplace.com/dogs/how-long-will-my-dog-live/page2.aspx

Kochan, Maureen. "America's Best Dog Parks." *Dog Fancy*, June 2008. pp. 38–39.

Mott, Maryann. "Puppies for Sale: What You Should Watch Out for When Purchasing a Pup Online." *Dog Fancy*, March 2008, p. 42.

Mott, Maryann. "Puppy Myths." *Dog Fancy*, September 2008, p. 56.

Pet Education: Dog Articles
http://www.peteducation.com/index.cfm?c=2

"Reproduction in Dogs and Cats."
http://animalpetdoctor.homestead.com/Reproduction.html

Ross, John, and Barbara McKinney. *Adoptable Dog: Teaching Your Adopted Pet to Obey, Trust, and Love You*. New York: W.W. Norton & Company, 2003.

FIND OUT MORE

Web Addresses
ASPCA: Dog Care
    http://www.aspca.org/pet-care/dog-care/
Dog Articles—All About Dogs
    http://www.i-love-dogs.com/dogsarticles.html
Dog Owner's Guide: Your New Puppy
    http://www.canismajor.com/dog/tpuppy.html
Puppies for Sale—Puppy Care, Breeds, & Health Information
    http://www.dogchannel.com/puppies/default.aspx
The Puppy Place—The Best Resource for Information, and FAQ's
    about Seeing Eye Dogs, Guide Dogs, Puppies, and Puppy Raising
    http://www.thepuppyplace.org
"Welcome to Healthypet.com!"
    http://www.healthypet.com/library_list.aspx?ID=1

GLOSSARY

authority (ah-THAR-ih-tee)—The power to enforce rules; the one in charge.

bond—Something that unites or binds individuals.

groomer—Someone who is paid to bathe, clip, and make dogs clean and neat.

hyperactive (hy-per-AK-tiv)—Having a lot of energy.

Invisible Fence®—A brand name for an electric fence that can be buried in your yard.

neutered (NOO-terd)—Removed a male dog's sex organs.

reproduce (ree-proh-DOOS)—To make babies.

responsible (ree-SPON-suh-bul)—Trustworthy.

spayed—Removed a female dog's sex organs.

vaccinations (vak-sih-NAY-shuns)—Medicine given as shots to prevent diseases.

veterinarian (vet-ruh-NAY-ree-un)—An animal doctor.

weaned (WEEND)—Able to eat solid food; no longer dependent on mother's milk.

INDEX